CARVING A FRIENDSHIP CANE

WITH TOM WOLFE & HIS FRIENDS

Text written with
and photography by
Douglas Congdon-Martin

TOM WOLFE'S
STEP-BY-STEP
CARVING INSTRUCTIONS
WITH A GALLERY OF
23 CARVINGS
BY SOME OF AMERICA'S
LEADING CARICATURE
CARVERS.

Schiffer
Publishing Ltd

77 Lower Valley Road, Atglen, PA 19310

CONTENTS

Printed in China

ISBN: 0-88740-891-5

Library of Congress Cataloging-in-Publication Data

Wolfe, Tom (Tom James)
    Carving a friendship cane with Tom Wolfe and his friends/text written with and photography by Douglas Congdon-Martin.
        p.   cm.
    ISBN 0-88740-891-5 (pbk.)
    1. Wood-carving. 2. Staffs (Sticks, canes, etc.)
I. Congdon-Martin, Douglas.
TT199.7.W637   1996
736'.4--dc20   95-52703
                                                          CIP

Published by Schiffer Publishing, Ltd.
77 Lower Valley Road
Atglen, PA 19310
Please write for a free catalog.
This book may be purchased from the publisher.
Please include $2.95 postage.
Try your bookstore first.

We are interested in hearing from authors
with book ideas on related subjects.

INTRODUCTION

The idea for the cane in this book came from my good friend and fellow carver Claude Bolton. We both belong to the Caricature Carvers of America, and the group was looking for some way to honor Ted McGill, a friend of our organization. Claude hit upon the idea of a cane made up of many segments which would be carved by the members of the CCA. Directions were sent to each member detailing the size of the block and the hole that was to be drilled through the center for assembly. The simple instruction was to be creative. In the gallery of this book you will see the results of their enormous talents.

In the first part of the book I will take you through the process of creating a four-face segment for a cane. What you learn there can be applied to any of your caricature carving or can be used to create your own friendship cane, by yourself or in your carving club.

The materials are simple. You will need to turn the base of the cane and the top. If it is to be the length of a walking stick, as ours was, you may also wish to turn a handle that will come about one quarter of the way down the shaft. The dowel is 5/8" in diameter and the segments are carved from blocks that are 2" x 2" x 3" with a 5/8" hole down the middle.

I wish to thank the members of the CCA for agreeing to have their work appear in this book. At the time of this publication they include: Jack Price of Texas; Peter Ortel of New York; Steve Prescott of Texas; Harley Schmitzen of Minnesota; Rich Wetherbee of Colorado; Bob Travis of California; Dave Dunham of Texas; Dave Stetson of Arizona; Keith Morrill of South Dakota; Joe Wannamaker of Illinois; Tex Haase of New Mexico; Doug Raine of Arizona; Marv Kaisersatt of Minnesota; Dave Rasmussen of Minnesota; Harley Refsal of Iowa; Harold Enlow of Arkansas; Claude Bolton of Texas; Gary Batte of Texas; Desiree Hajny of Kansas; Pete LeClair of Massachusetts; and Randy Landen of Kansas.

I hope you enjoy this book as much as we have in creating it. The cane you create will be a true token of friendship. The fruits of your creativity and skill will be cherished by the recipient for many years to come.

CARVING THE CANE

There are several ways to approach the blank. I can carve a single head in the round, two faces, or one face on each corner for a total of four. This will be a four-faced segment. At the bridge of the nose I cut a stop...

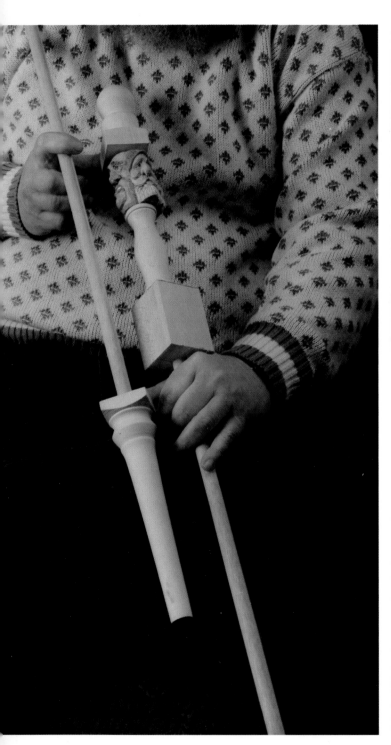

The idea for a friendship cane came to us from our good friend, Claude Bolton. It is a great way for a bunch of carvers to do something to honor one person. The stick is built on a 5/8" dowel. The cap, handle, and foot are turned, and the segment blanks are 2" x 2" x 3", with a 5/8" hole down the middle.

and come back with a wedge cut to take it out.

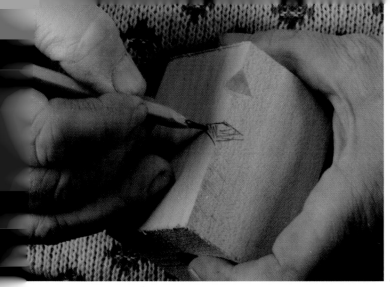

The bottom of the nose goes straight in and then angles out along the lip.

Deepen the wedge.

As with the bridge, cut in under the nose...

I want a wide triangle for the nose, so I come up from the back of the nose to almost the center of the eyes, leaving just a little bridge.

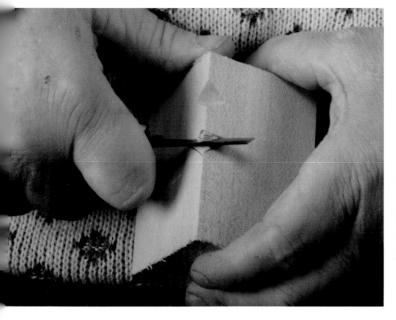

and back to it from the lip.

Cut along the surface of the nose...

5

and cut off the wedge along the line of the nose.

Cut the back corner of the nostril at a forty-five degree angle.

It doesn't take much imagination to see the whole face taking shape around the carved nose.

Follow the line of cheek and cut down along the back of the nostril.

Continue the line of the cheek down into the chin.

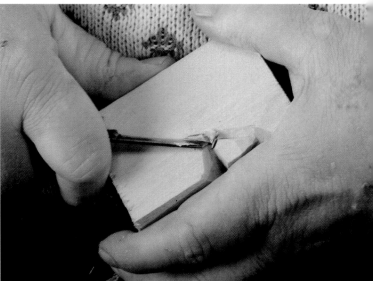

Cut back to the cheek line from the lip...

to create a smile line in the cheek. Repeat on the other side.

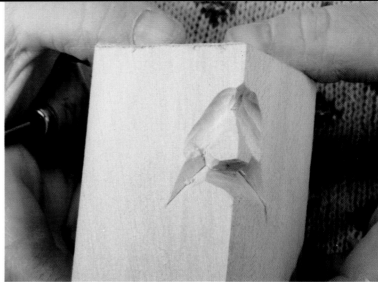

begins to form the contour of the eye area.

Soften the cheek line with a half round gouge.

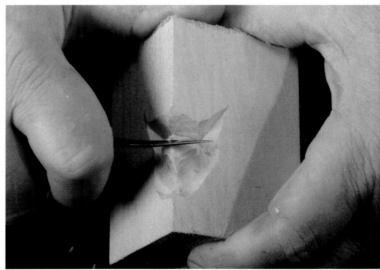

Knock the sharp edges off the nose, to kind of round it up.

Coming down from the eye socket on the same line...

The result.

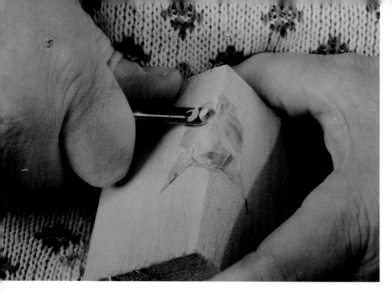

With a gouge, widen and deepen the eye sockets.

Now is a good time to define the area of the four faces, so I don't overlap them. Do this by drawing a center line on each side.

Progress. This sets the character for the face.

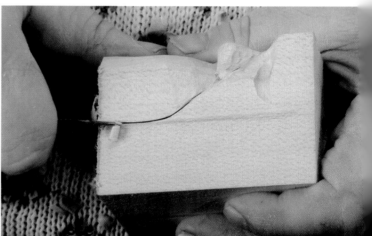

Carry the line of the moustache around to the sides, and down to the bottom.

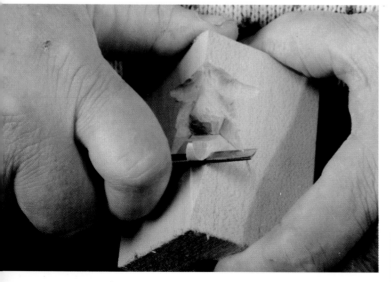

I think I'm going to give this guy a big walrus moustache that covers up almost everything below his nose. I begin by knocking off the corner beneath the nose.

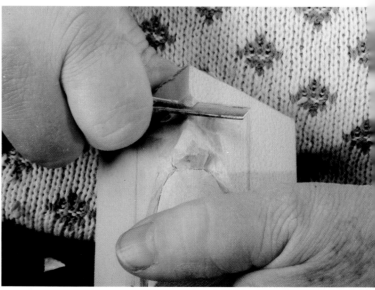

Knock off the point of the forehead.

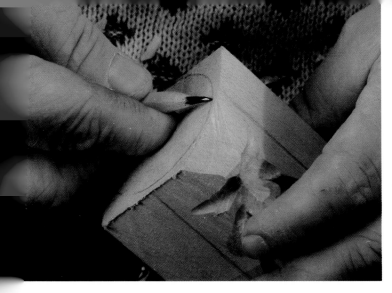

I draw a ring around the top to show how deep I want to go. I want to leave a large enough surface for good contact with the adjoining segment of the cane.

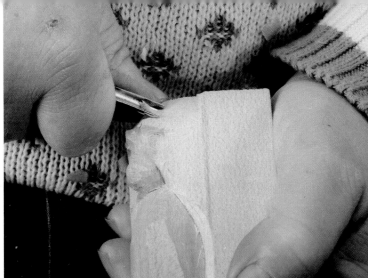

Also carry a channel above the eye brow to bring it out.

Gouge between the eyebrows to create a separation.

Blend the channel into the top of the head.

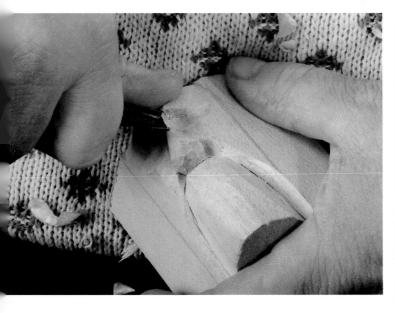

From the separation use the gouge to carry the line into the eye socket.

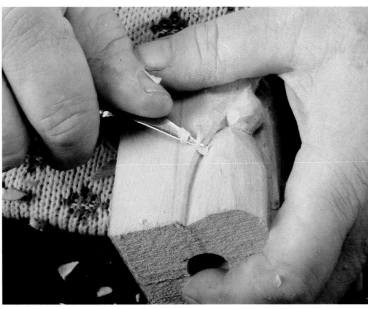

Go over the face and soften up the real hard lines.

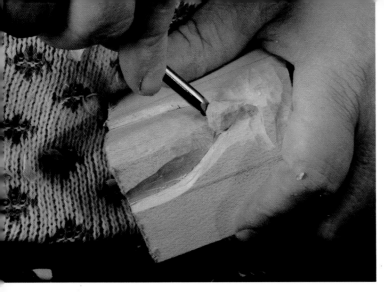

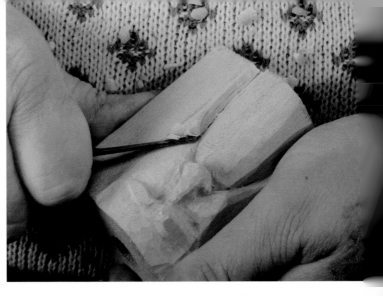

Cut straight in with a small half round gouge to create the nostrils. You don't want them to touch in the middle.

Shape the contour of the cheeks, cutting down one direction...

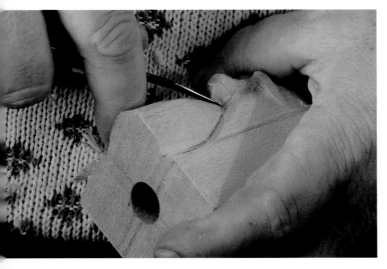

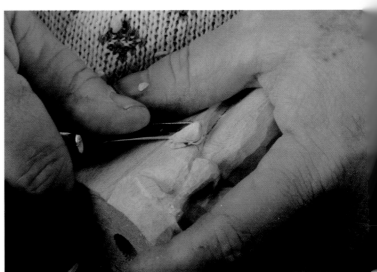

With a knife, clean up the nostril.

and up the other.

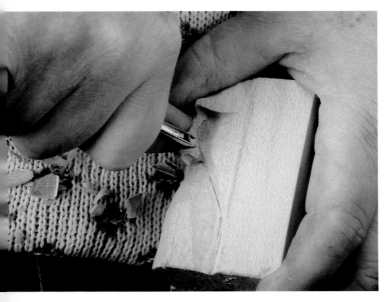

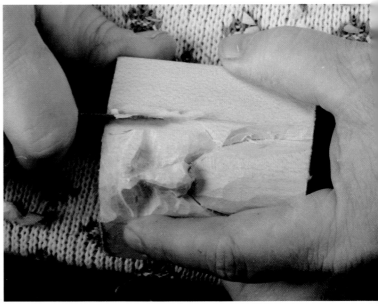

With a gouge, cut up and over the top of the nostril, letting the cut break off at the cheek.

Continue the contouring into the temple.

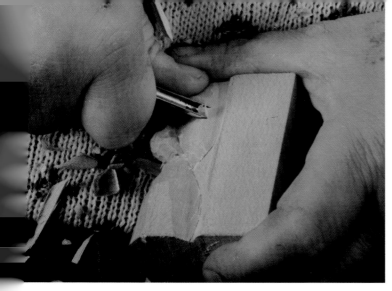

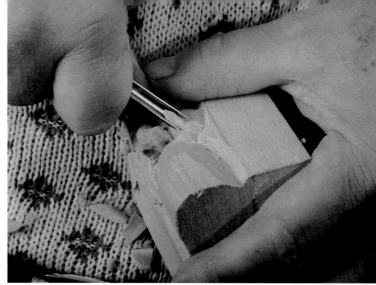

The face needs narrowing at the temples, so I carry the eye line around to the sideburns with a gouge.

By carving the cheek line I give the face a little more action.

Blend it in with a knife.

Progress. He is getting a frowning look, so I think I will go with it, get rid of the moustache and give him a beard.

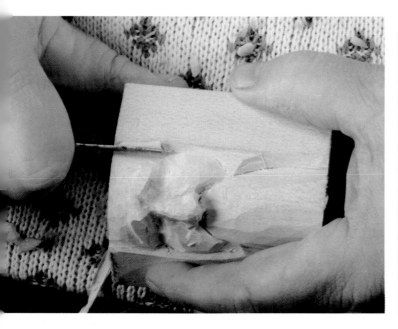

Thin the forehead.

Draw the line of the lips.

Cut into the line at 45 degree angles from the top...

The bow of the lip is created by cutting in with a flatter gouge along the surface of the upper lip...

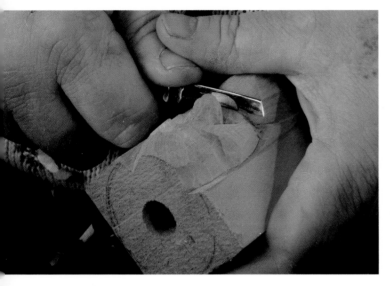

and the bottom.

and cut off the shaving with a knife.

Create the separation in the upper lip (the philtrum) with a small half-round gouge, coming right up to the center of the nose.

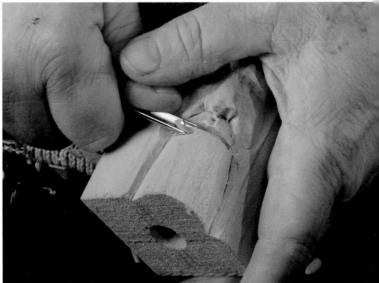

With #9 gouge cut a channel under the lower lip to bring it out.

Progress on the mouth.

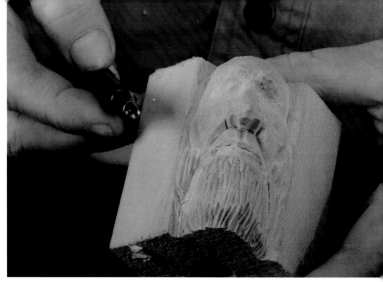

The eyepunch has one edge ground down.

Cut the major lines of the beard with a veiner. The lines of the beard should not be straight, and should run toward the mouth. If you don't do that, his coffee won't run down his chin.

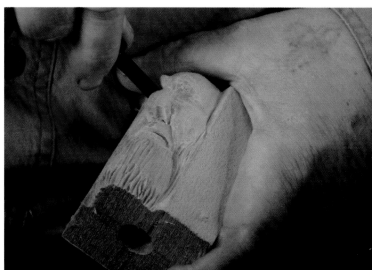

Pick the right size, put it in place and rock it back and forth...

Ready for the eyes.

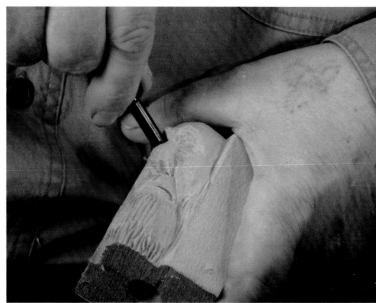

and up and down.

Do the other side.

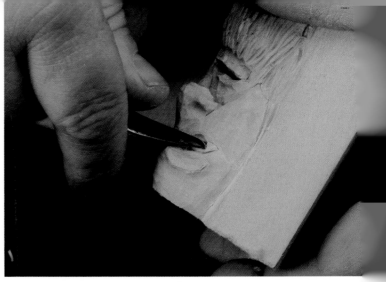

Then, with the blade flat against the eyeball, push it back in the corner to pop out a nitch.

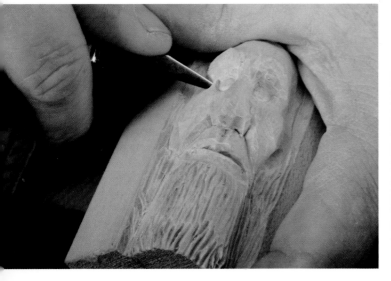

On the outer corner of the eye, run you knife along the line of the upper eyelid...

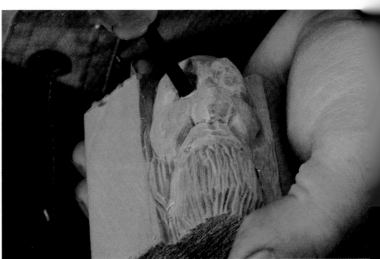

With a smaller eyepunch, create a pupil inside the iris. This line is mainly to hold the paint.

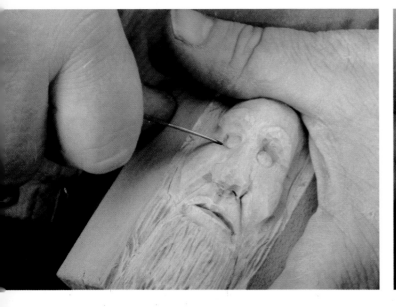

and the lower eyelid.

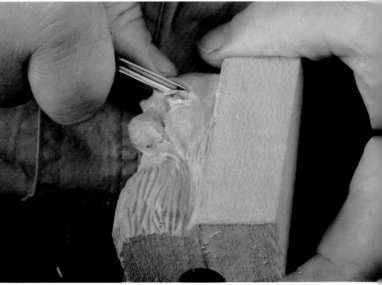

With a veiner, come over the eye to create the upper lid.

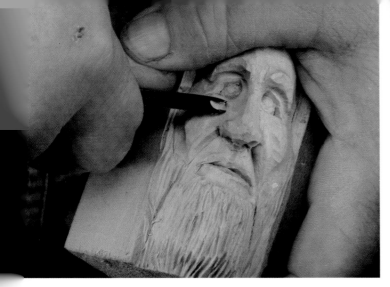

Holding the tool flat on the downward edge, create some bags under the eyes.

Ready for painting.

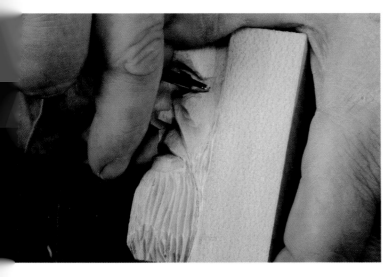

With a smaller veiner dress up the ends of the eye. Here I'm creating a little crow's foot.

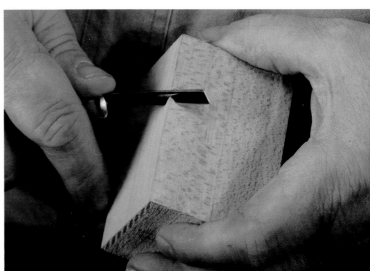

The next corner is opposite the first. I am starting the bridge of the nose about halfway down, cutting in at the brow...

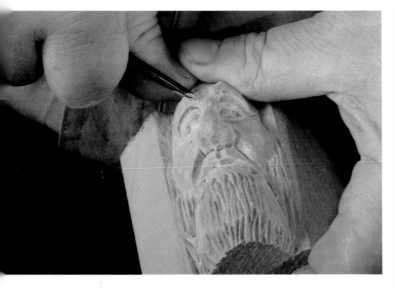

Use the same tool to create the hair of the eyebrows. I kind of work these lines back toward the nose for a realistic look.

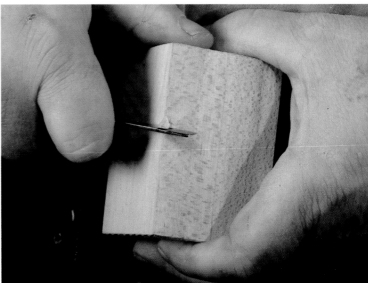

and back to it from the nose.

Cut straight in at the bottom of the nose...

Progress.

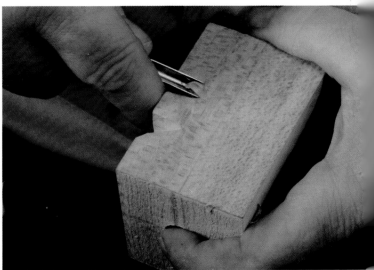

and back to it from the lip. You always want to make this a little wider than you think it should be.

Shape the eye sockets with the gouge. When doing this, make sure you can see both corners of the gouge above the wood. This will keep you from tearing up the wood.

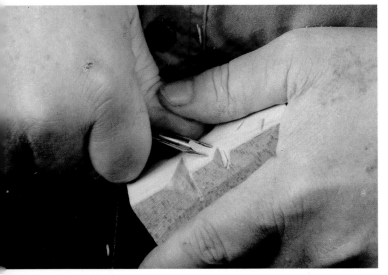

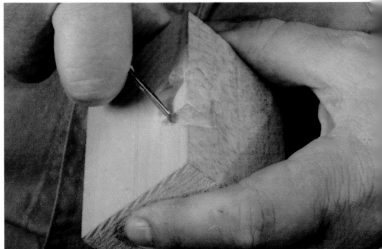

This time I'm going to cut from the corner of the mouth to the nose with a gouge, following the cheek line.

Use the three cuts to trim off the back of the nostril flange, as you did on the first face.

Round the nose down.

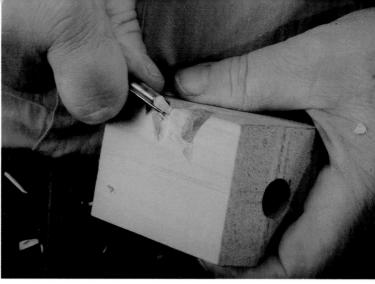

With a half round gouge, separate between the eyebrows.

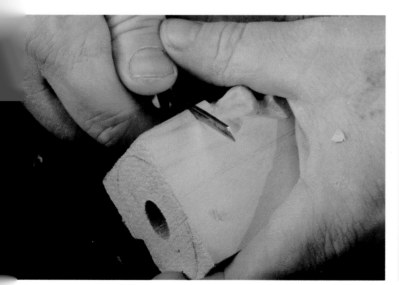

This guy will have a cap, so I make a stop above the eyebrows...

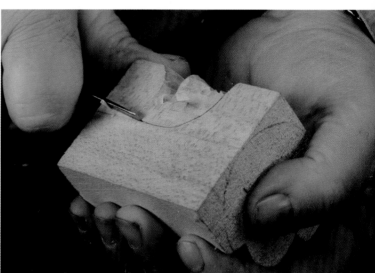

Carry the line of the cap around the side of the head and down to the beard line.

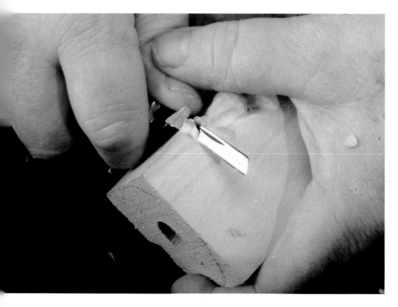

and come back to it from the forehead.

Cut the face back to the cap line.

Cut the nostrils with a gouge...

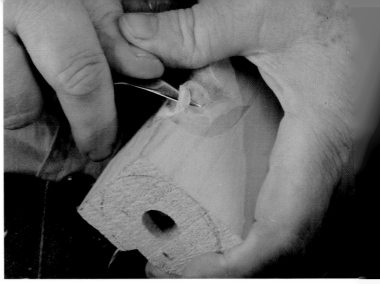

I want a round tip to the nose, so I visualize it and dish the surface of the nose above the tip.

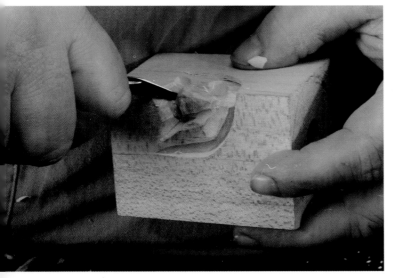

and nip the wood off with a knife.

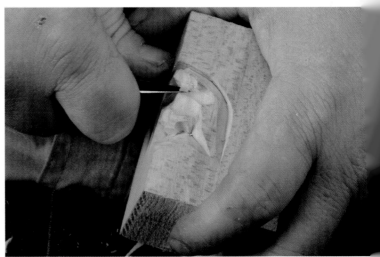

Round the edge of the dishing cut.

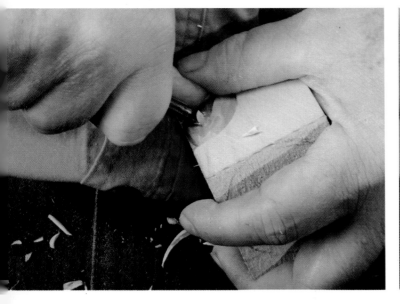

Come over the nostril flange with a gouge, breaking it off at the cheek line.

Create another channel between the ball of the nose and the nostril flange.

The result is a little bit of a ski-jump nose.

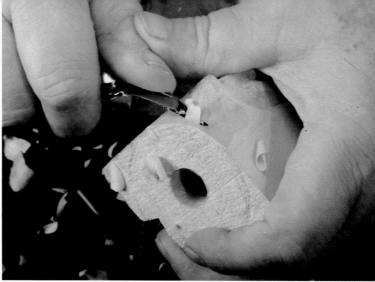

Round the cap.

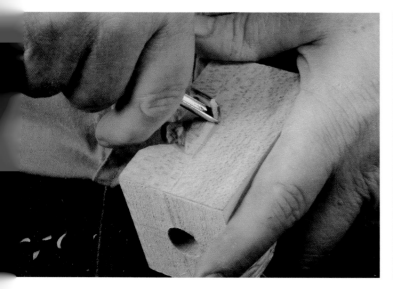

Carry the eye sockets around to the temple.

Continue the line of the cap down to the bottom of the side of the face.

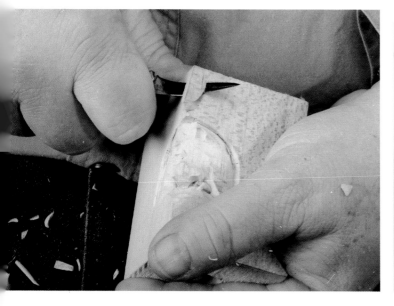

Starting a little bit above the edge of the cap, so you leave a rim, knock off the corner of the cap.

With the cup of a gouge against the cheek, round it down to the moustache line.

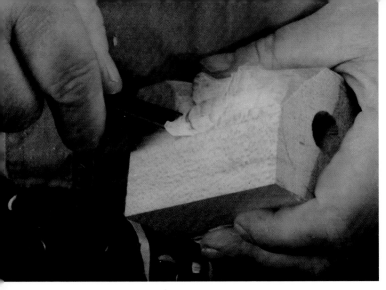

With the same tool, clip off the bottom of the shaving.

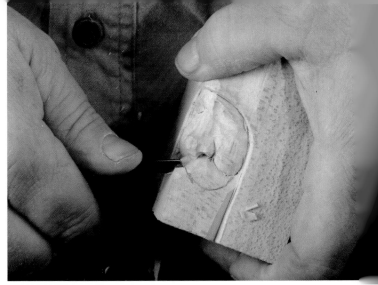

Cut a stop down and in on each side of the moustache separation...

The curve of the gouge, gives a nice upturn to the moustache and roundness to the cheek.

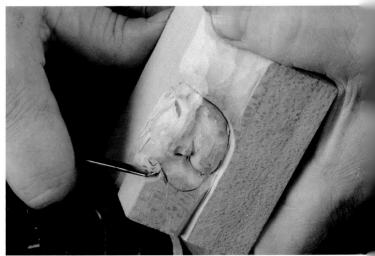

and cut away the area between.

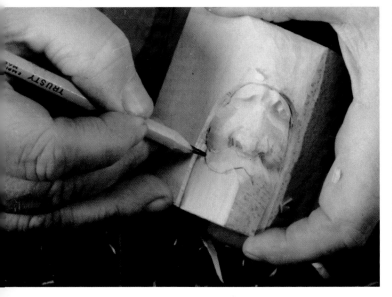

Draw the lower edge of the moustache.

Follow the lower line of the moustache with the same gouge as earlier, cup side down. Move out to the end of the moustache.

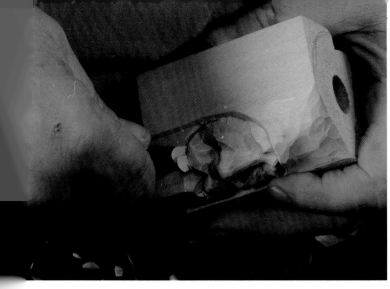

With the same gouge, cup side out, come up to the moustache from the beard.

Trim off the shaving with a knife.

Round the beard over.

Make a v-cut to create the part line between the two sides of the moustache.

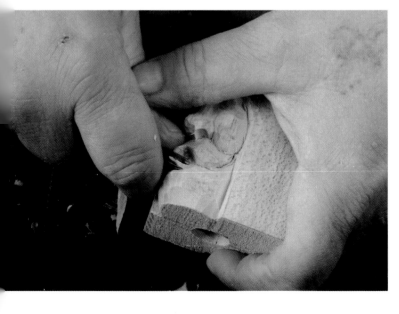

Go across the lower chin with a gouge, to bring out the lower lip.

Ready for the eyes.

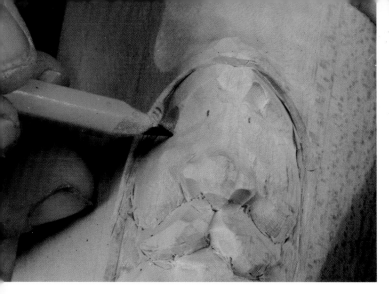

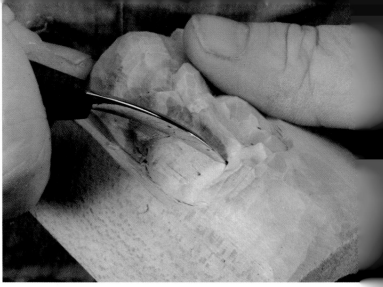

In this face I will carve an eye, instead of using the eyepunch. First I draw dots where I think the inside of the eye should go.

and down.

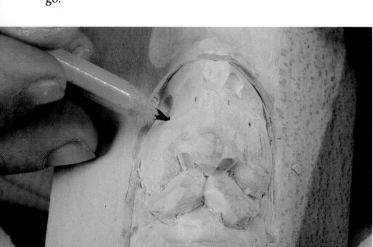

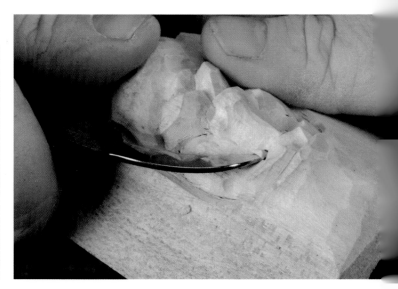

Two more dots define the outside corners.

and then cut back into the corner from the eyeball to pop out a nitch.

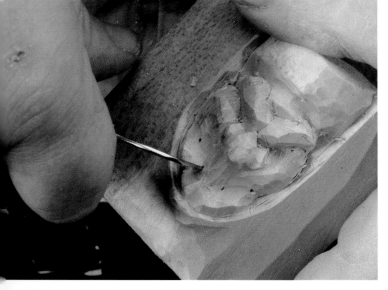

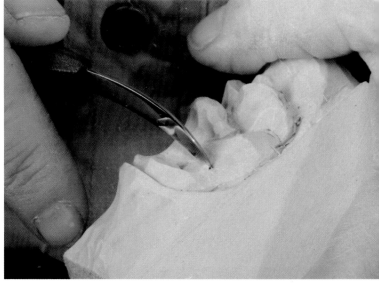

Cutting at about a 45 degree angle, begin at the inside corner and cut up...

Repeat on the outer corner first along the lower lid...

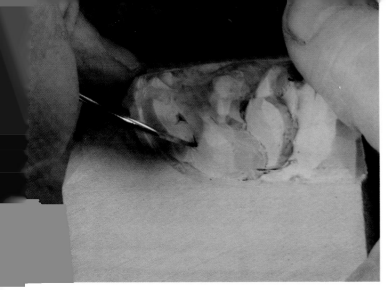

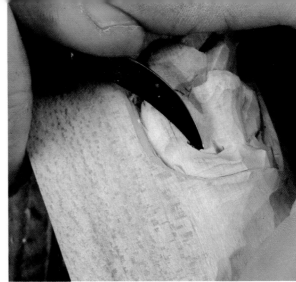

then along the upper, and then pop out the nitch...

Carefully round the eyeball to the lids.

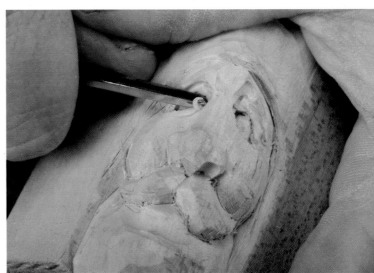

for this result.

Go under the lower eyelids with a veiner to create baggy eyes.

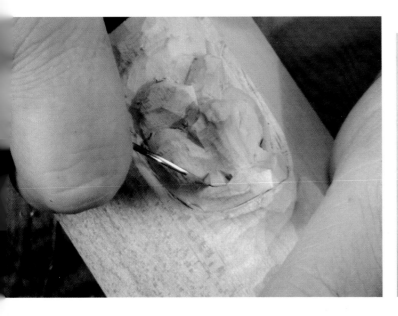

Now simply connect the lines of the lids across the top and bottom of the eyes.

Go over the upper lids with a veiner as on the first face for this result.

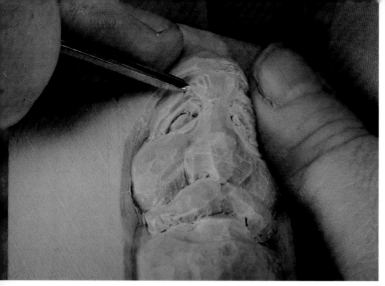

With a small veiner carve the hairs of the eyebrows...

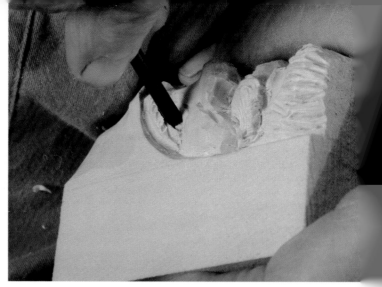

Use a small eyepunch to create the iris in each eye.

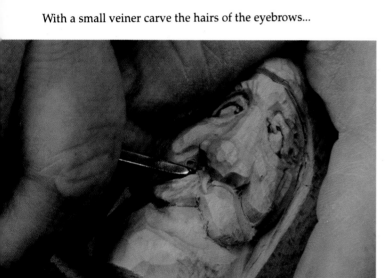

the moustache...

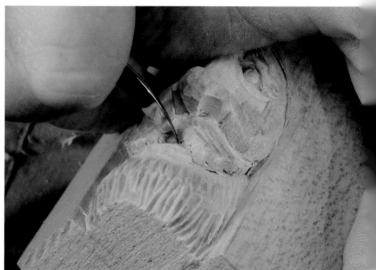

Clean out the mouth leaving the ridge of a tooth line.

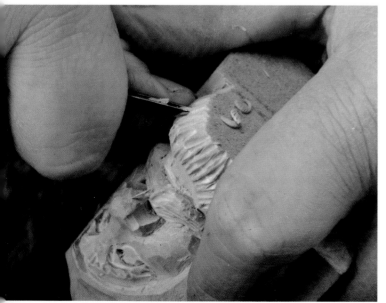

and the beard.

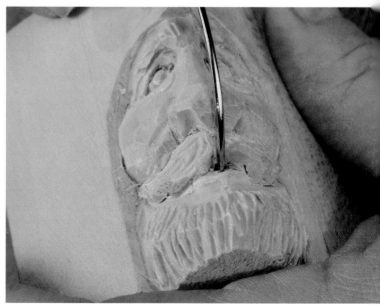

Separate the teeth...

and back to it from the nose.

and the second face is finished.

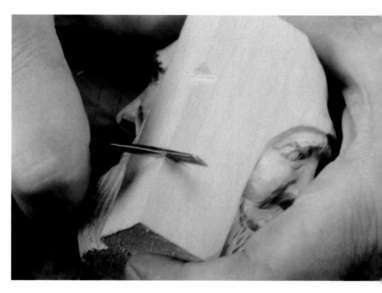

This figure will have a big nose. I put a stop way down here....

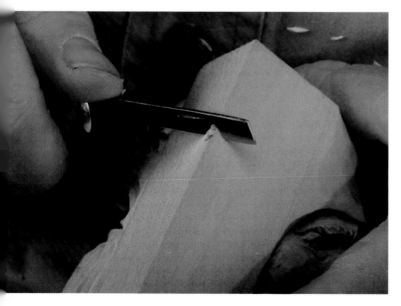

The bridge of the nose on the third face is between the first and second. Cut in on the brow....

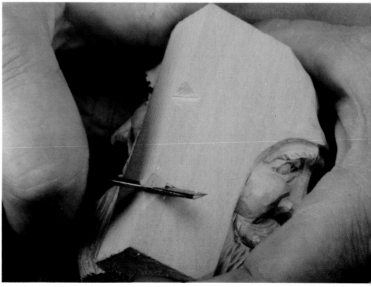

and cut back to it from the lip.

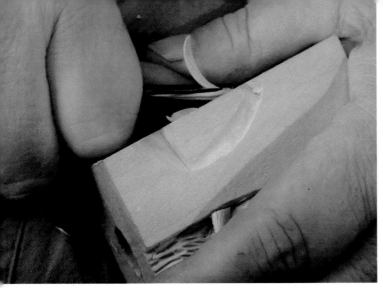

From the corner of the mouth cut back to the bridge of the nose...

down the cheek line...

for this result.

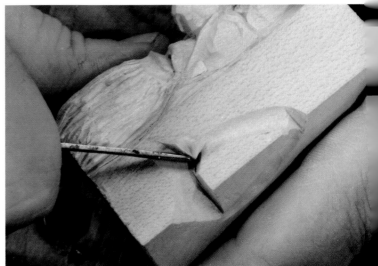

and back to the nose from the lip, lifting out the triangular nitch.

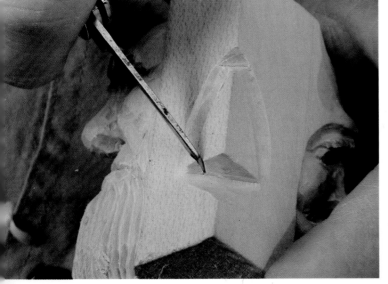

Remove the back corners of the nose, cutting across the nostril flange...

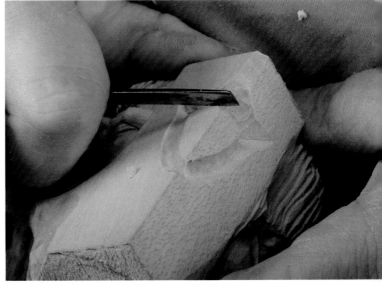

Round off the nose.

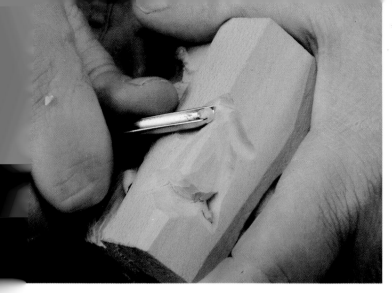

Widen the area of the eye socket.

Cut the underside of the bangs...

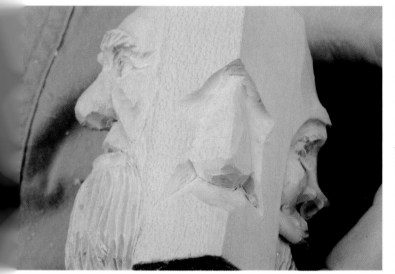

This will take you to about here.

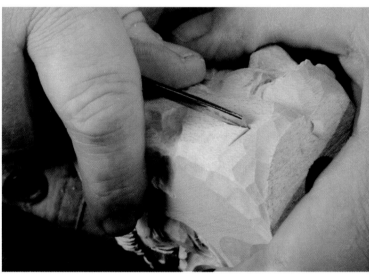

and the hair at the side of the head, meeting at the part.

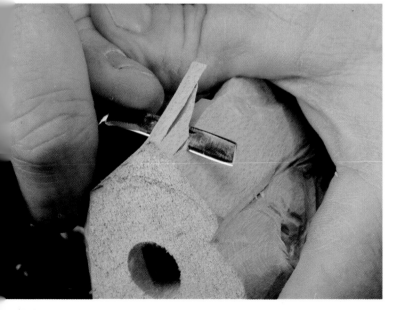

Beginning with the corner, round the forehead up and over.

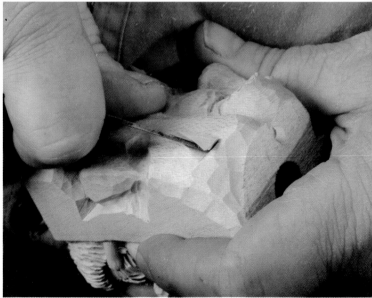

Cut back to the point from the forehead.

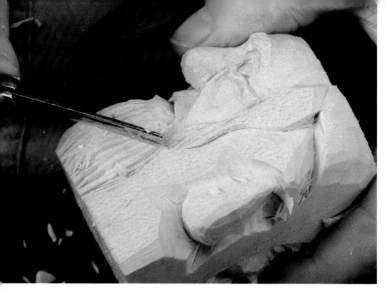

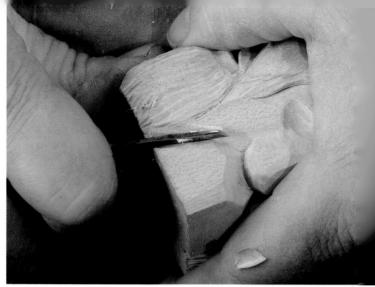

Continue the line of the hair down the face, so its sideburn shares with the hair of the beard in the next figure.

Trim back to it from the moustache.

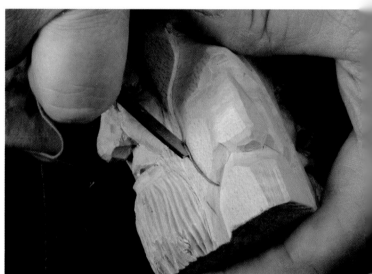

Bring the other hair line down, so it blends with line of the side figure's cap.

I want the cheek to come to this line, and the hair to run the other side of it. Cut a stop...

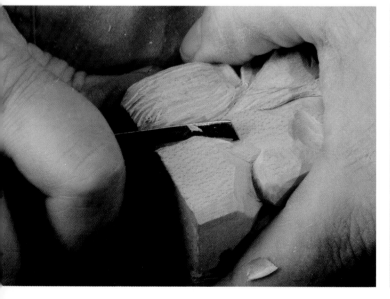

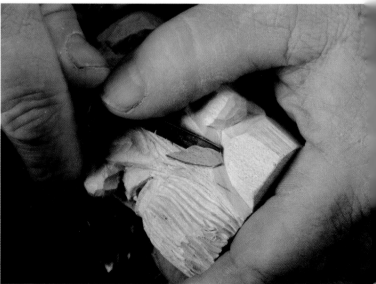

Bring the cheek line down along the moustache line.

and trim back to it from the cheek.

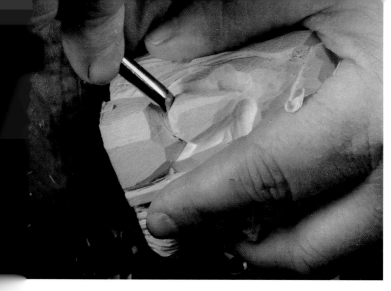

Add the nostrils to the nose.

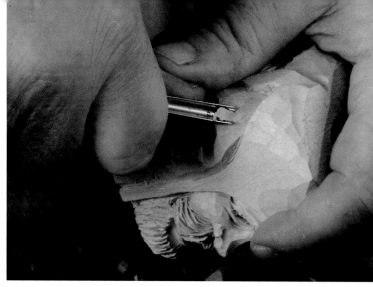

Make the separation between the brows.

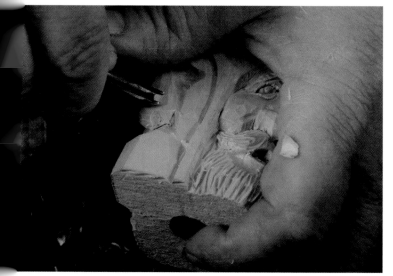

Gouge above the nostril flange.

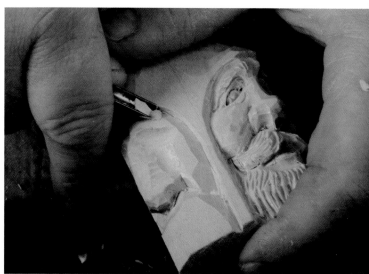

Bring a channel over the top of the eyebrows to make them bushier.

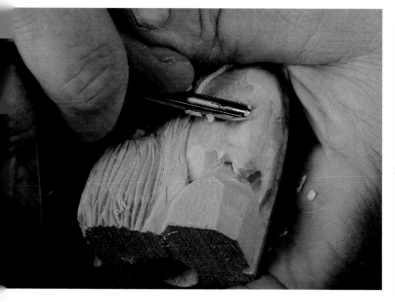

Blend things in. I want to leave him with a big ol' Roman nose.

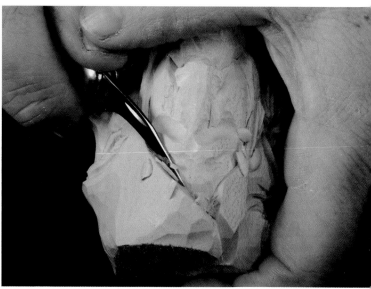

Clean and blend the forehead and eyebrow contour.

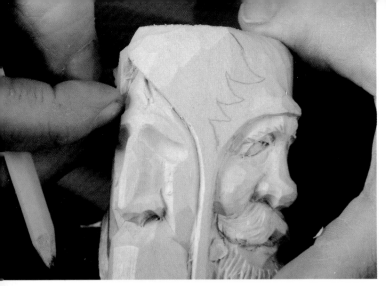

I'm going to let this figure's hair overlap the next figure's cap.

This ties the two figures together.

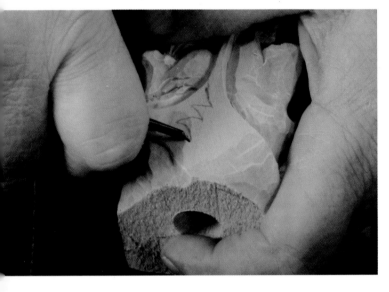

Cut stops around the outline of the hair, deeper where the hair comes together.

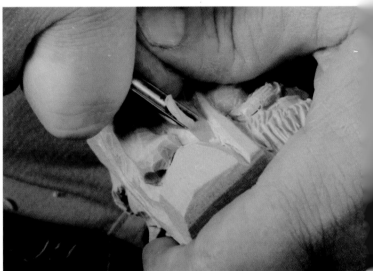

Add some character lines along the face.

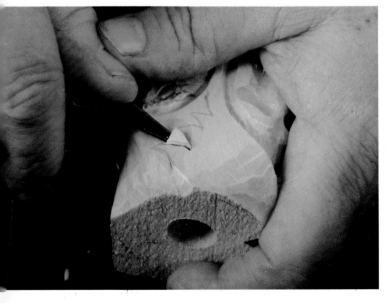

Come back into the V and lift out the wood.

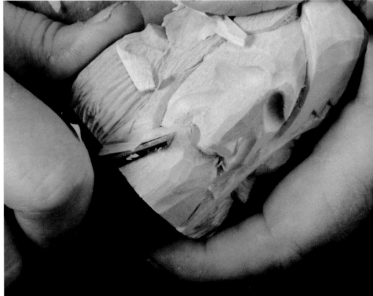

Round the area of the moustache.

30

Cut a long V to separate the moustache at the center.

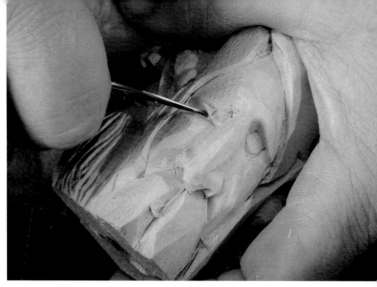

Cut the corners of the eyes, first along the upper lid, then along the lower lid, then over the eyeball into the corner.

Carry the eye sockets back into the temples.

With a gouge go across the top of the lid to bring it out...

With the larger nose, I will use a larger eyepunch for the eyes. Push it in and move it up and down, and side to side.

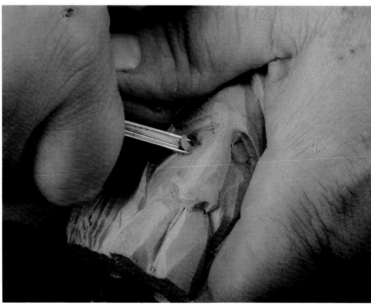

and across the bottom to create a bag under the eye.

31

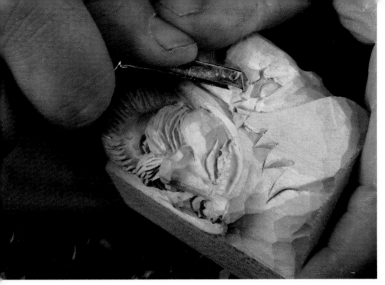

With a knife, clean up the carving.

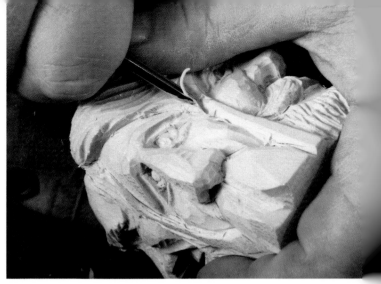

A smaller veiner creates more hair detail on the ends of the hair...

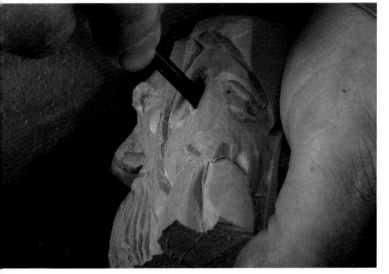

With a smaller punch, add an iris.

...the moustache

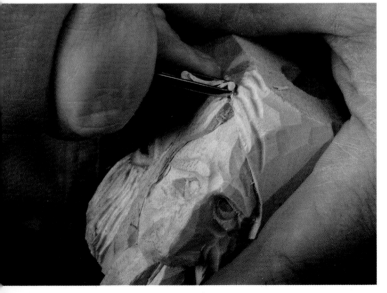

A veiner is used to create hair lines in the scalp and moustache.

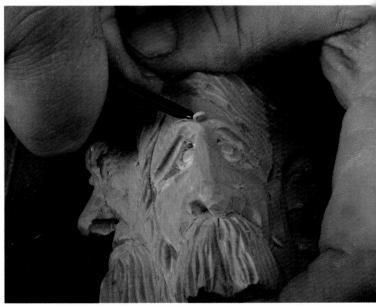

...and the eyebrows.

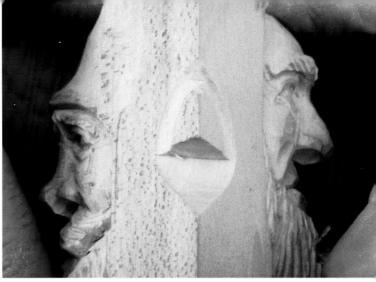

Continue with the nose as on the other faces. This is smaller, but flows from the other faces. You don't want one face radically different from the others.

Finished.

Round the nose and open up the eye sockets.

On the last side find a spot between the bridges of the two adjoining sides and cut a bridge.

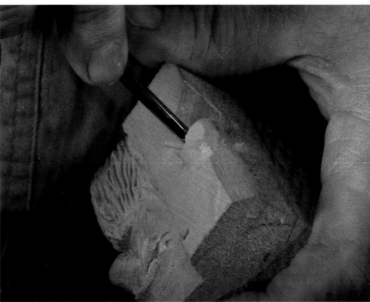

Add the nostril. With a smaller nose, I need a smaller nostril.

33

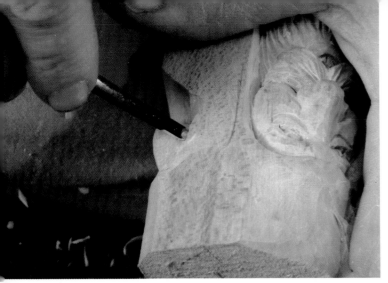

Come over the top of the nostril flange with same gouge.

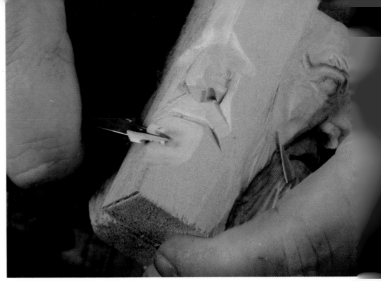

Clean up a place for the open mouth.

Separate the eyebrows.

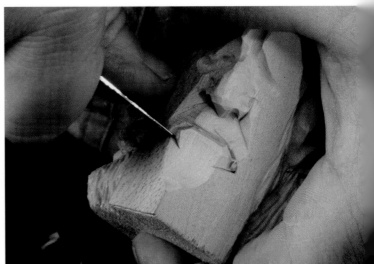

Open up the corners of the mouth.

This figure will have an open mouth. Cut a stop for it here.

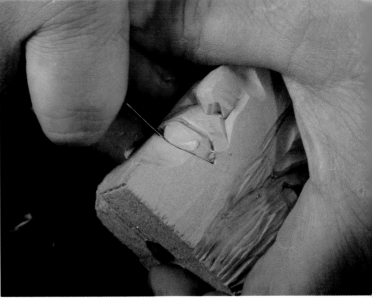

Cut a stop in the top of the bottom lip...

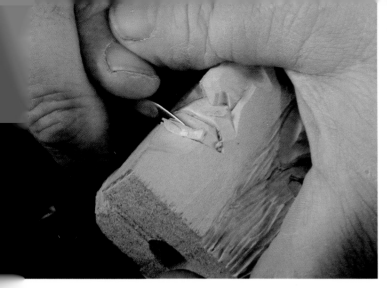

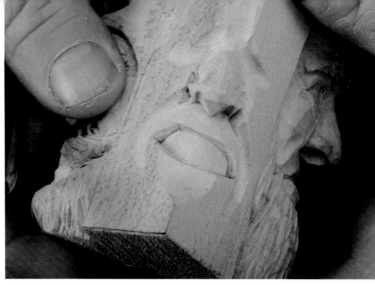

and cut back to it from the mouth.

The result.

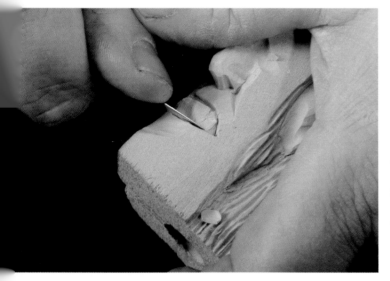

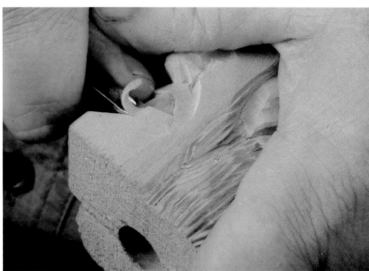

I reduce the wood in the mouth so I can make teeth out of it.

Continue underneath the bottom lip.

Come down from the side of the nose on both sides of the mouth with a gouge, to create some lines.

Cut the philtrum at the center of the upper lip.

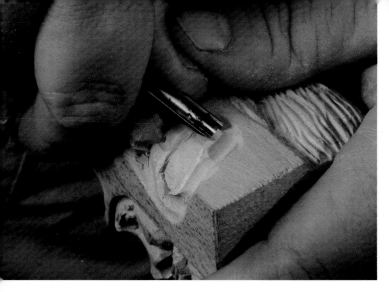

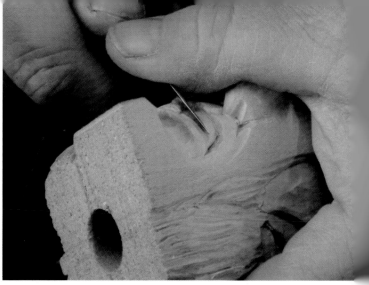

Cut the corner of the bottom lip so it has the appearance of going under the upper lip at the corner.

Make a fine line to separate the upper and lower teeth.

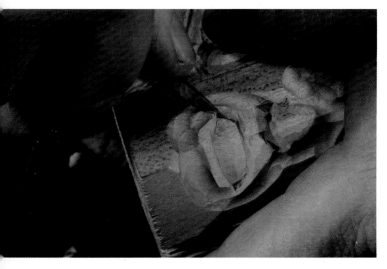

To turn the mouth down a little bit I extend the line of the upper lip into the corner...

Cut a stop between the top front teeth...

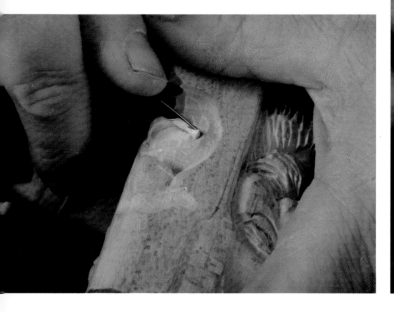

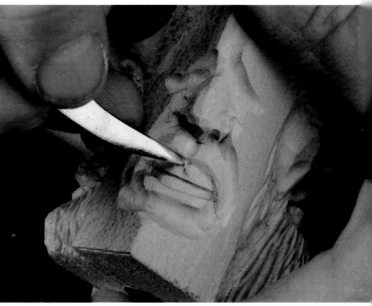

and cut back to it from below.

and slice back to it from both sides.

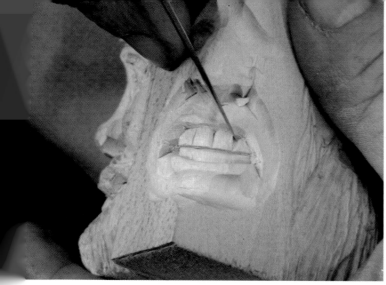

Form the teeth on the sides in the same way.

Teeth to do a dentist proud.

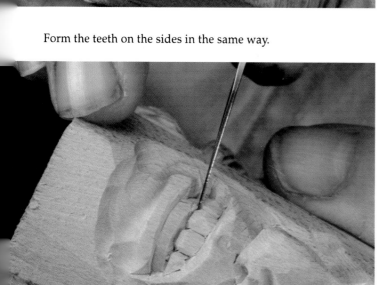

Cut a little teeny bit of the corners of each tooth.

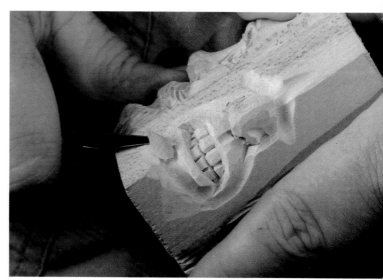

Contour the jaw on either side of the chin.

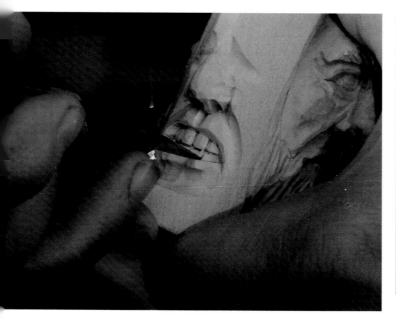

Do the bottom teeth in the same way.

This guy's hair will part right in the middle. Cut one side of the part...

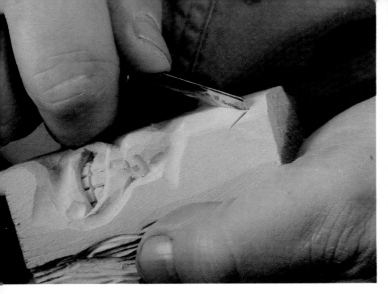 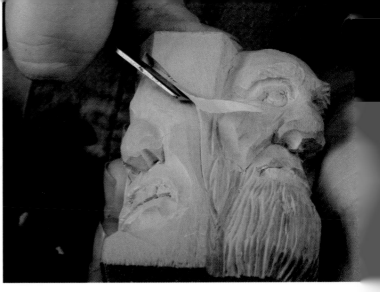

and the other...

Cut back to the stop from the face.

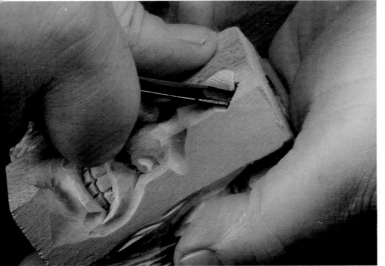 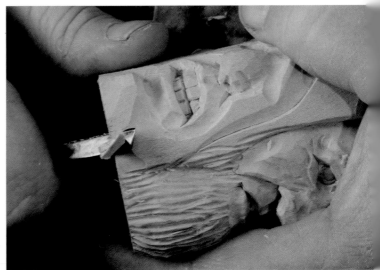

and come back between them.

Round up the chin.

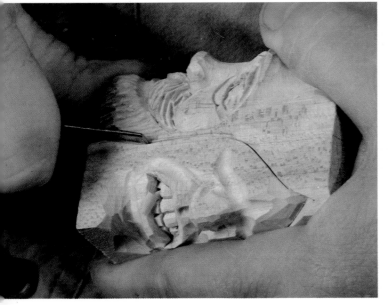 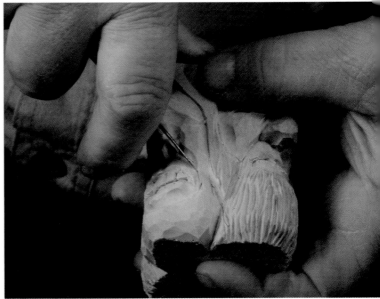

Carry the hairline down the side of the face.

The character lines around the face need deepening.

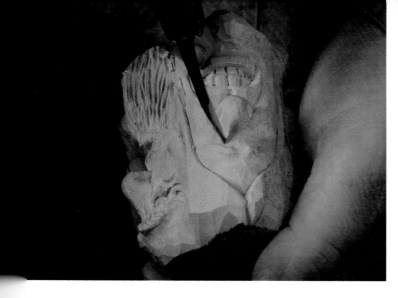

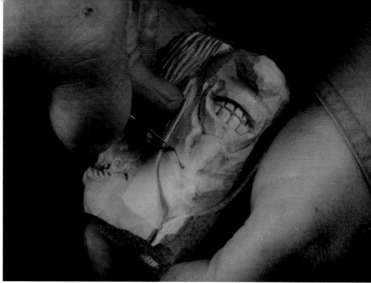

To make squinting eyes, I make a small downward cut at the inside corner of the eye...

Continue the line of the eye cut to the end of the eye...

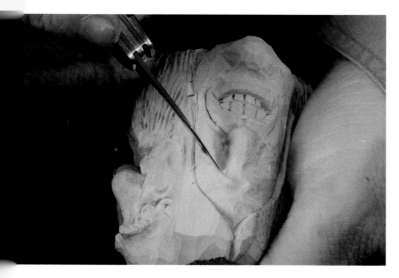

Starting at the same point cut a little longer cut along the line of the eye itself.

and cut back to it from below.

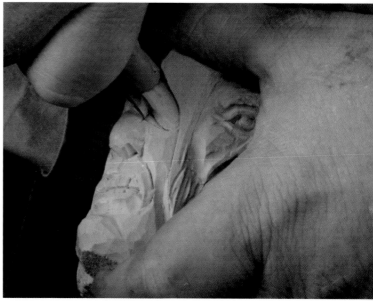

Cut back into the corner formed by the first two cuts and take out the nitch.

Cut a stop on the lower lid...

39

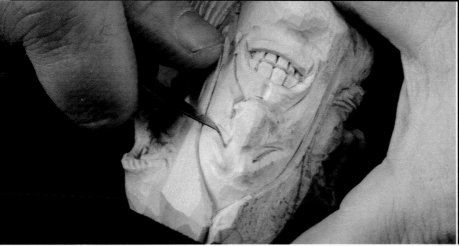

and come back to it from the eyeball.

The result.

With a veiner add bags under the eyes.

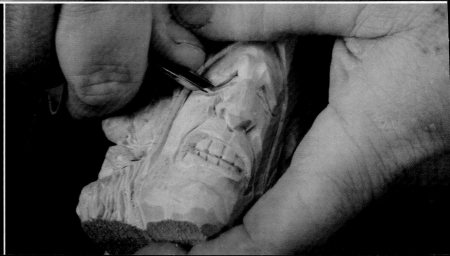

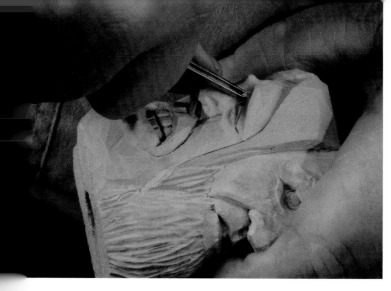

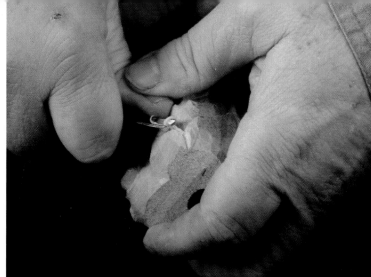

With a smaller veiner add the folds of the lids above the eyes. Come up the inside, stop, turn...

Add the hair lines with a v-tool.

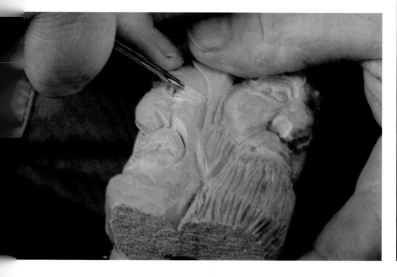

and come down the eyelid.

Continue with the eyebrow hair.

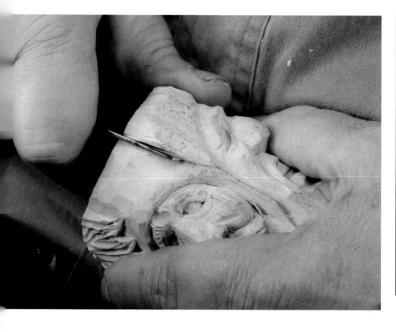

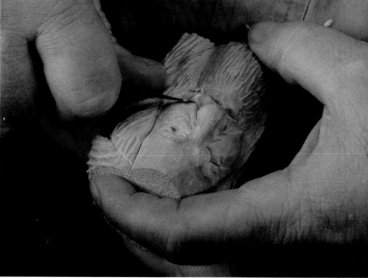

I need to separate between the hat and the hair.

Go back over the whole thing, tying the faces together, and generally cleaning up the carving.

Ready for painting.

PAINTING THE CANE

For wood carving I use Winsor and Newton Alkyd tube paints. For most coats the paints are thinned with pure turpentine to a consistency that soaks into the carving, giving subtle colors. What I look for is a watery mixture, almost like a wash. In this way the turpentine will carry the pigment into the wood, giving the stained look I like. It has always been my theory that if you are going to cover the wood, why use wood in the first place. It should be noted that with white, the concentration of the pigment should be a little stronger. I use some pigments right from the tube to add some dry brushed highlight colors.

I mix my paints in juice bottles, putting in a bit of paint and adding turpentine. I don't use exact measurements. Instead I use trial and error, adding a bit of paint or a bit of turpentine until I get the thickness I want.

The juice bottles are handy for holding your paints. They are reclosable, easy to shake, and have the added advantage of leaving a concentrated amount of color on the inside of the lid and the sides of the bottle which can be used when more intense color is needed.

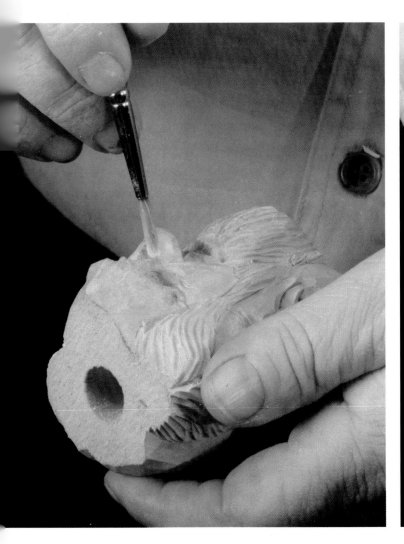

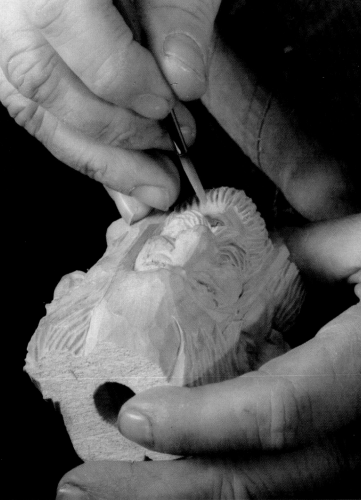

Paint all the areas that have no hair with a flesh toned mixture of white with raw sienna, and a little touch of red.

Touch a mixture of red and flesh on the lips...

the nose...

Where shadows appear, add some raw burnt sienna.

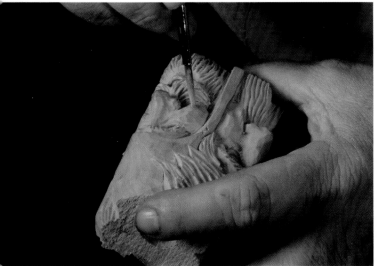

the cheeks...

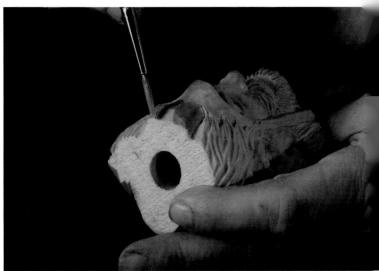

Add blue to the cap.

and around the eye. Blend it out.

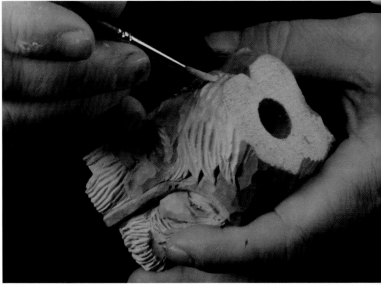

Some of the characters will have blond hair. Begin with yellow...

and go over it burnt sienna to soften it into blond.

The blond and the brown compliment each other side-by-side.

The result of burnt sienna over yellow.

The last figure will have gray hair. This gray is from my wash bottle..."waste not, want not."

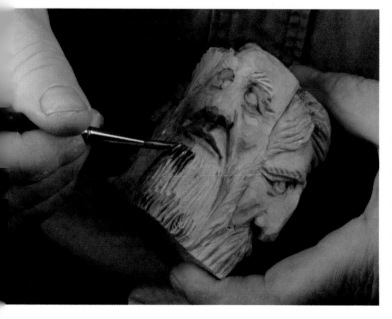

Here I'll put down the burnt sienna for brown hair.

Let the hair set for awhile before adding highlights.

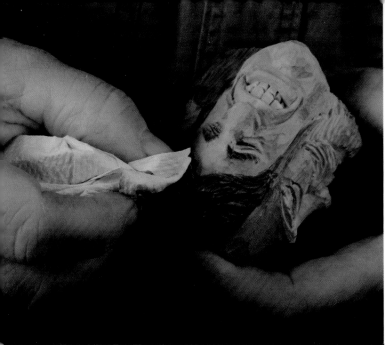

When I know I'm going to dry brush something, I wipe it down while the first coat is wet. This takes up the excess and knocks the paint off the high points where the dry brush will go.

Where teeth are showing add some white.

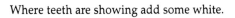

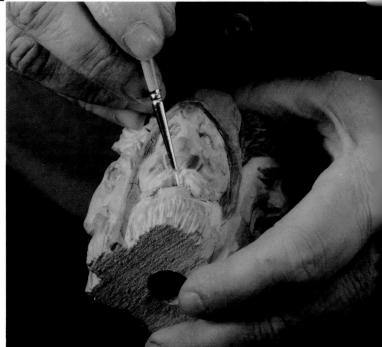

Progress.

Brown eyes begin with burnt umber. Paint the iris.

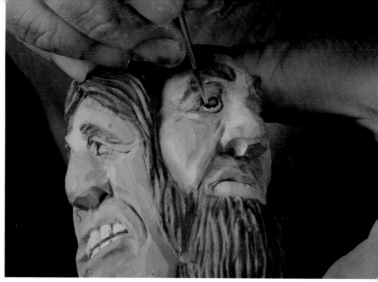

With a dry brush I blend the white with the brown, leaving the rim dark. Keep drying your brush and blending.

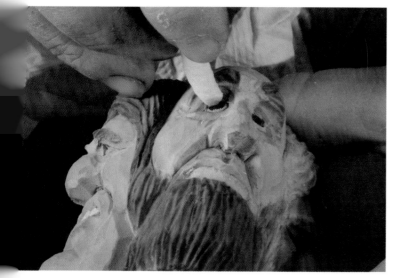

Absorb some of the turpentine back out of the eye with the corner of a piece of paper towel.

A little burnt sienna on top of the white brings some life into the eyes.

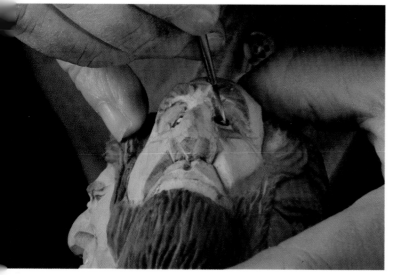

I want to leave the rim of the iris dark umber, but in the center of each I put a dot of white.

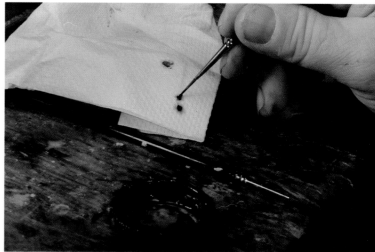

The pupil is a dot of black paint. Before applying it, I gently touch the brush to paper towel to pull some turpentine out of the paint.

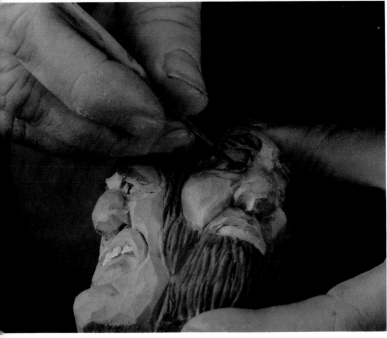

Paint the pupil.

A white glint is applied. To get the accuracy I need, I am using a piece of wood carved to a point, but a bamboo skewer seems to work best. The glint needs to be in the same position and attitude on each eye.

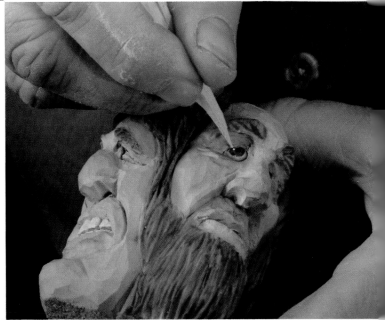

The result.

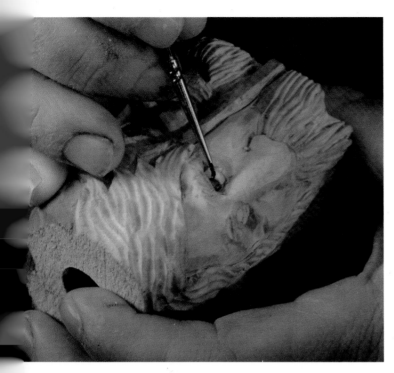

The blond figures get blue eyes. I start with a darker blue.

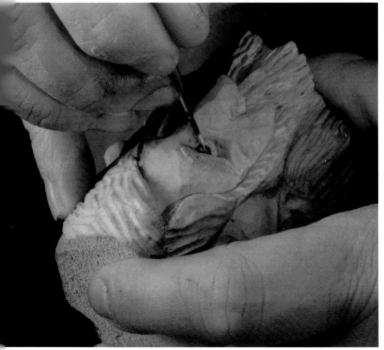

Dry brush some white into the blue at the center of the iris.

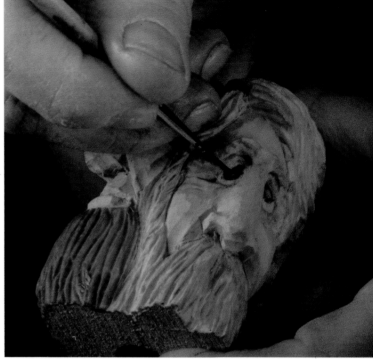

Add a dot of black for the pupil...

and a speck of white for highlight for beautiful blue eyes.

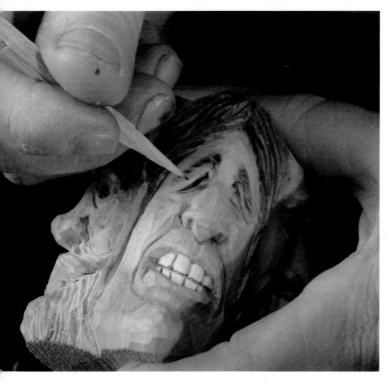

In the squinter I'm just going to add a dot of black to the eyelid, mixing it with a little white to create a shadow.

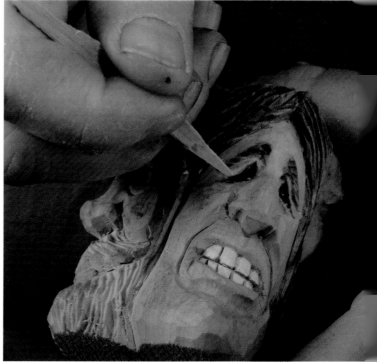

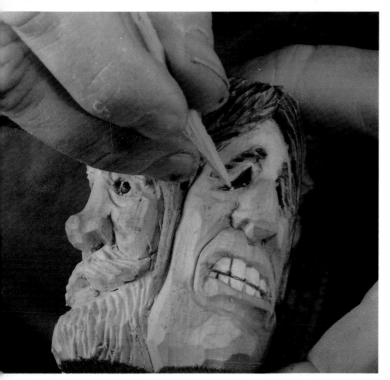

In the slit put a dot of white at each side of the iris...

and some raw sienna between them.

The result.

Finally dry brush some white in the gray hair of the squinter. I pick up pure paint from the neck of the paint bottle on a fluffy dry brush. Work most of the paint out on a piece of wood.

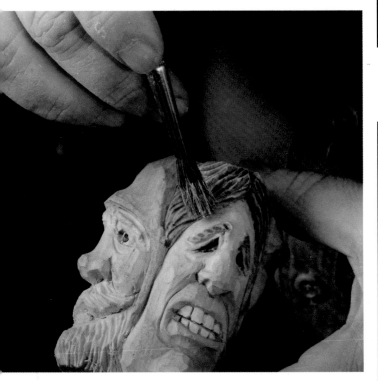

You might also wish to add highlights to the beard of the next character.

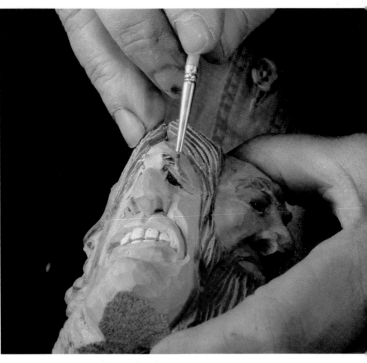

Go lightly over the hair so the high points pick up the white paint. The first application will probably not be noticeable, but as you continue, the hair will pick up highlights.

Do the eyebrows too.

Finished.

FRIENDSHIP CANE GALLERY
INTRODUCTION
BOB TRAVIS

The gallery features the work of Tom and twenty-one of his friends from the Caricatures Carvers of America (CCA). Contrary to the normal flow of things in the publishing world, we did not set out to do this project with a book in mind. Rather, our intent was to carve a cane for a friend and we would like to share that story with you. Before doing this though, perhaps a few words about CCA would be appropriate.

Back in the fall of 1990 a group of caricature carvers met in Fort Worth, Texas to discuss the possibility of forming a national organization to promote our common interests. As the discussion began it soon became apparent that our primary goal was to promote the art of caricature carving within both the woodcarving community and the general public. To attain this goal we have embarked upon an ambitious program which includes exhibitions, seminars, and pubications on caricature carving. Because of the logistics of projects of this nature, we made the difficult decision to restrict the membership in CCA to 25 carvers. Imagine for example, the energy that would have been expended in organizing this project if we had several dozen members. As of this writing CCA membership stands at 22 ans we are pleased that each member contributed to the cane. Naturally, when Tom suggested that the CCA Cane Gallery be added to this book, we readily agreed.

The cane was carved for Ted McGill. Our group meets annually to have fun, carve a little, and plan a few activities for the coming year. Ted attended a couple of these meetings as Tom's guest. The chemistry was good, and we all enjoyed his company. Shortly after the first meeting Ted surprised us with a beautiful set of color photographs chronicling three days of fun. Then, the next year each of us received a great 3-hour video tape of our activities. So, this cane represents our humble attempt to say thank you to a friend. We appreciated the photographs and the video, but most of all we appreciate the friendship of Ted McGill.

Harley Schmitzen carved this relief segment.

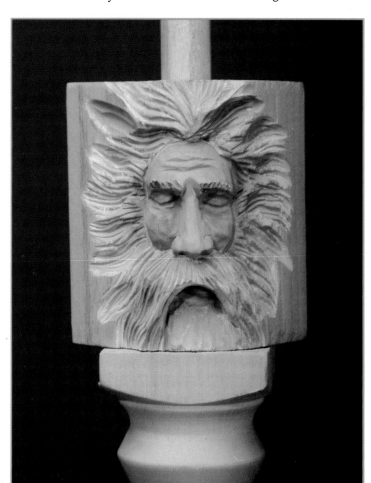

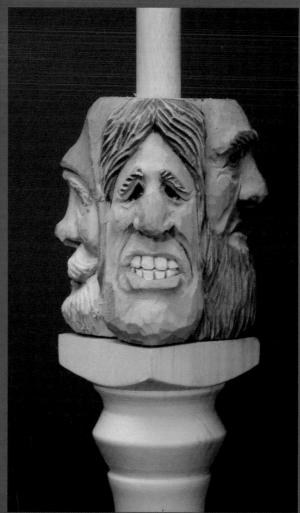

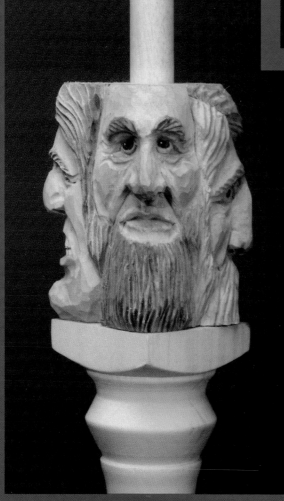

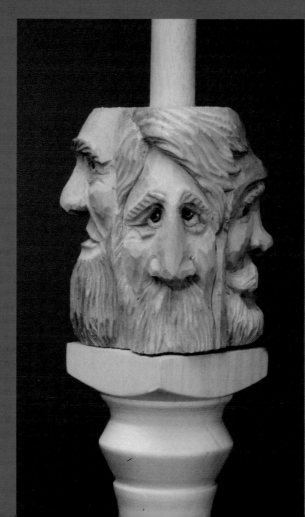

Four-faced segment by Tom Wolfe

Two-faced holiday combination by Doug Raine.

"The President and Her Husband,"
two-faced segment by Joe
Wannamaker.

Dave Dunham's two-faced segment.

In-the-round segment by Tex
Haase.

In-the-round segment by Keith Morrill

Rich Wetherbee's character in-the-round.

Peter Ortel's public servants make up this two-faced segment.

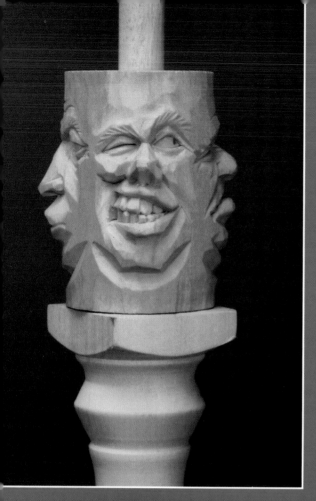

Harold Enlow created this four-faced segment.

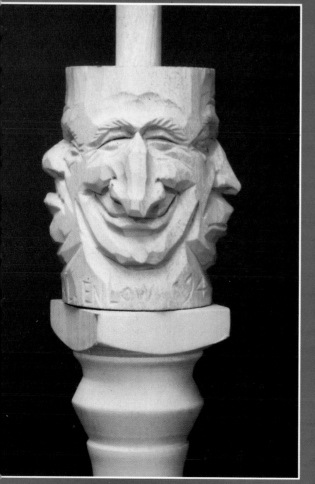

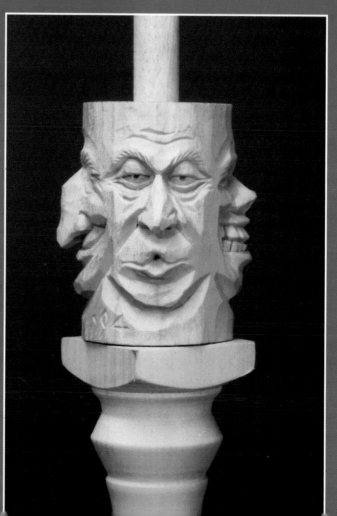

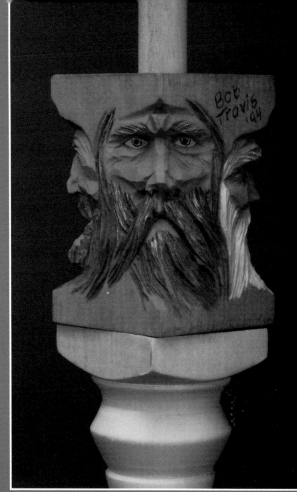

A four-faced segment by Bob Travis.

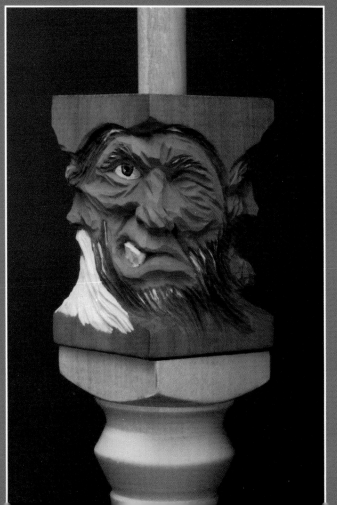

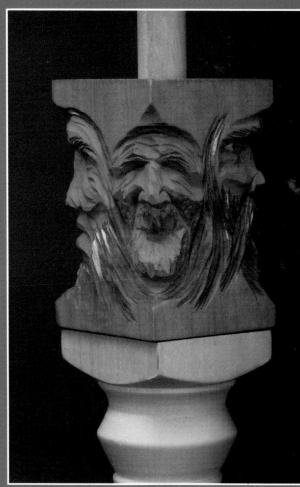

An in-the-round segment by Dave Rasmussen.

Randy Landen created this ghoulish Santa segment.

This squat fellow is by Marv Kaisersatt.

In-the-round segment by Dave Stetson.

Two toothful faces in this segment by Gary Batte.

Steve Prescott offered this two-faced segment.

Claude Bolton created this four-faced segment.

Four of Jack Price's little people hold up this segment.

Desiree Hayjny offers this raccoon in-the-round.

Harley Refsal's in-the-round figure.

The clown in the box make a nice segment. This one is by Pete LeClair.

These four faces by Tom Wolfe
include humans and an animal face.